John 3:16

Jesus and Nicodemus in Jerusalem

Jim Reimann
Illustrations by Julia Filipone-Erez

An important leader of the Jews named Nicodemus,
Secretly came late one evening to speak to Jesus.
"Rabbi, or teacher, we know it is from God you have come,
Because of all the amazing miracles you have done."

Jesus answered, "I tell you the truth—Amen and Amen,
To enter God's kingdom, a person must be born again."
"But how can someone like I am, who is now old and worn,
Return one more time to his mother's body and be born?"

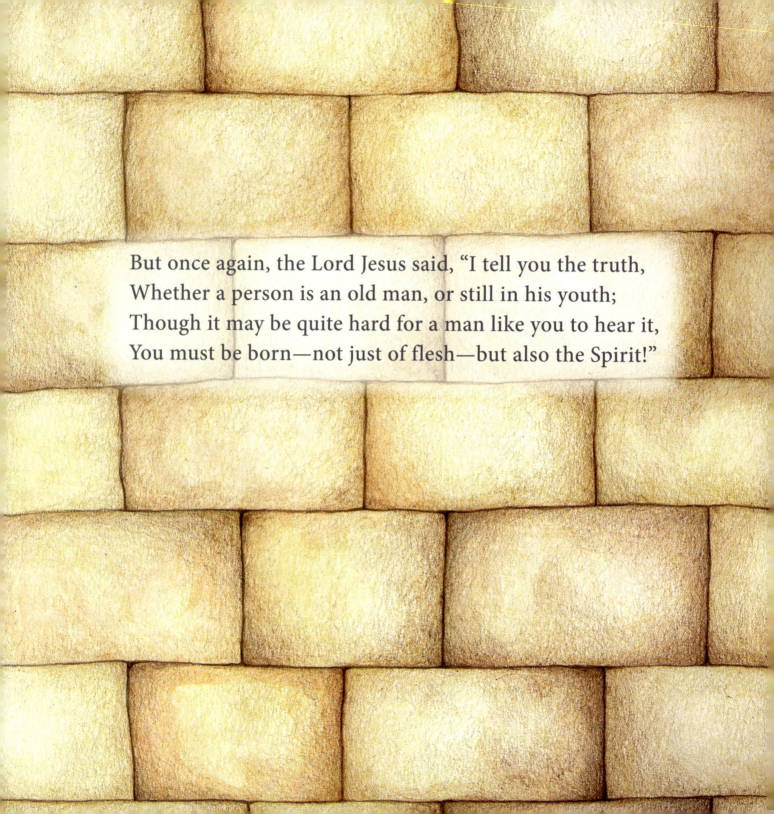

But once again, the Lord Jesus said, "I tell you the truth,
Whether a person is an old man, or still in his youth;
Though it may be quite hard for a man like you to hear it,
You must be born—not just of flesh—but also the Spirit!"

"Understand, flesh gives birth to flesh, and Spirit to spirit;
It is by faith you are saved, and will heaven inherit.
Being born from your dear mother is not nearly enough,
For salvation is by faith, not good works or other stuff."

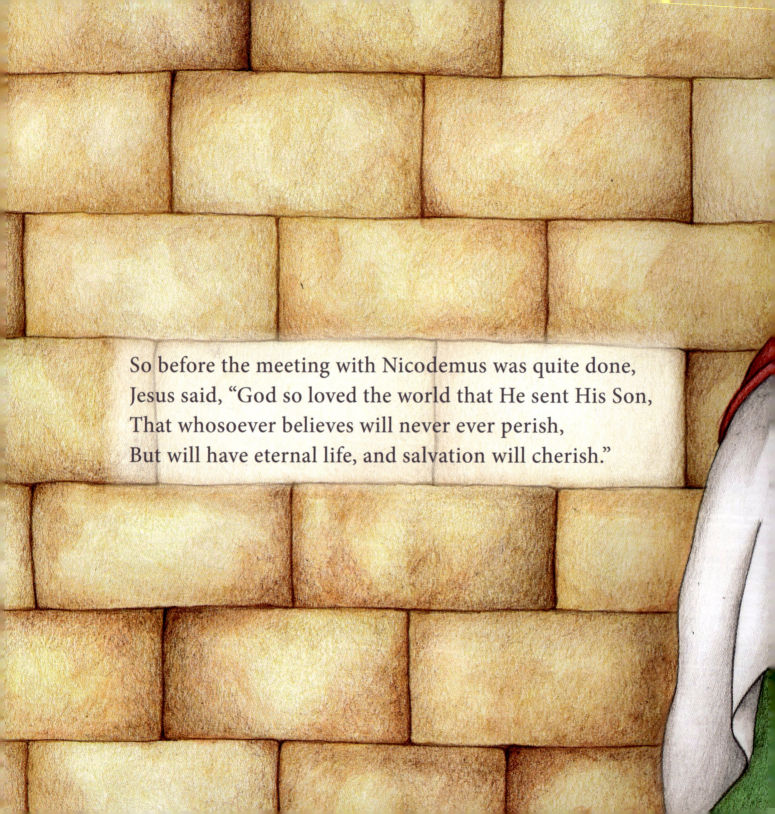

So before the meeting with Nicodemus was quite done,
Jesus said, "God so loved the world that He sent His Son,
That whosoever believes will never ever perish,
But will have eternal life, and salvation will cherish."

Little children, to be saved and someday go to heaven,
Whether your name is John or Jane, or Mary or Kevin,
Never trust in yourself, your works, or your good behavior,
But trust Jesus as Lord, your only hope, and your Savior.

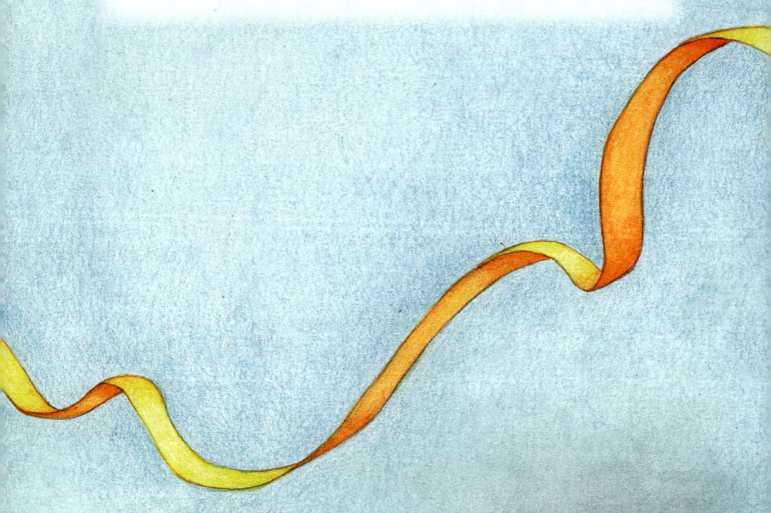

Copyright © 2012 Jim Reimann
www.JimReimann.com

Rev. Jim Reimann
Israel Tour Leader of 25+ Pilgrimages
Editor of the Updated Editions of:
My Utmost for His Highest (Oswald Chambers)
Streams in the Desert (Lettie Cowman)
Morning by Morning (Charles Spurgeon)
Evening by Evening (Charles Spurgeon)

All rights reserved. No part of this book may be used or reproduced by any means, graphic, electronic, or mechanical, including photocopying, recording, taping or by any information storage retrieval system without the written permission of the publisher except in the case of brief quotations embodied in critical articles and reviews.

ISBN: 978-965-7607-02-2

For ordering information, please contact the publisher:

Intelecty, Ltd.
76 Hagalil
Nofit, Israel 36001
Tel: 97249930922
Fax: 972722830147
amirarkind@gmail.com

Printed in the Holy Land